D1071408

# how i got that story

# how i got that story

*A Play In Two Acts*

## by AMLiN GRAY

NELSON DOUBLEDAY, INC.
*Garden City, New York*

© Copyright, 1981, 1982, by Amlin Gray
© Copyright, 1979, by Amlin Gray
AS AN UNPUBLISHED DRAMATIC COMPOSITION
All Rights Reserved

CAUTION: Professionals and amateurs are hereby warned that HOW I GOT THAT STORY is subject to a royalty. It is fully protected under the copyright laws of the United States of America, and of all countries covered by the International Copyright Union (including the Dominion of Canada and the rest of the British Commonwealth), and of all countries covered by the Pan-American Copyright Convention and the Universal Copyright Convention, and of all countries with which the United States has reciprocal copyright relations. All rights, including professional, amateur, motion picture, recitation, lecturing, public reading, radio broadcasting, television, and the rights of translation into foreign languages, are strictly reserved. Particular emphasis is laid upon the question of readings, permission for which must be secured from the author's agent in writing.

All inquiries concerning rights (other than amateur rights) should be addressed to Lois Berman, 250 West 57th Street, New York, N.Y. 10019.

The amateur production rights in HOW I GOT THAT STORY are controlled exclusively by the DRAMATISTS PLAY SERVICE, INC., 440 Park Avenue South, New York, N.Y. 10016. No amateur performance of the play may be given without obtaining in advance the written permission of the DRAMATISTS PLAY SERVICE, INC., and paying the requisite fee.

SPECIAL NOTE ON SONGS AND RECORDINGS

For performance of such songs and recordings mentioned in this play as are in copyright, the permission of the copyright owners must be obtained; or other songs and recordings in the public domain substituted.

MANUFACTURED IN THE UNITED STATES OF AMERICA

HOW I GOT THAT STORY was first presented by the Milwaukee Repertory Theater, John Dillon, Artistic Director, Sara O'Connor, Managing Director, on April 12, 1979. The play was directed by Sharon Ott, with set by Laura Maurer, costumes by Mary Gibson, lights by Ross Hamilton, sound design by Mark Van Hecke. The stage manager was Vito Zingarelli. The cast was as follows:

THE REPORTER　　　　　　　　　　　*James Pickering*
THE HISTORICAL EVENT　　　*Jack McLaughlin-Gray*

The play opened Off-Broadway at the Westside Arts Theater on February 18, 1982. It was presented by Harold DeFelice and Louis W. Scheeder with J.N.H. Ventures, Inc. and Margo Lion. The director was Carole Rothman, the set was by Patricia Woodbridge, costumes by Carol Oditz, lights by Pat Collins, sound design by Gary Harris, dance sequence by John Lone. The stage manager was Fredric H. Orner. The cast was as follows:

THE REPORTER　　　　　　　　　　　*Don Scardino*
THE HISTORICAL EVENT　　　　　　*Bob Gunton*

*This play is dedicated to Sharon Ott*

# CHARACTERS

THE REPORTER. An eager young man in his late twenties

THE HISTORICAL EVENT. The actor playing this part appears at times as the entire EVENT, at other times as people who make up parts of the EVENT, as follows:

THE DEPUTY COORDINATOR
MR. KINGSLEY
AN AMBONESE PEDESTRIAN
A BONZE
MADAME ING
A STREET URCHIN
A G.I. IN MIMI'S FLAMBOYANT
LIEUTENANT THIBODEAUX (Pronounced "TIH-buh-doe")
PFC PROCHASKA
A GUERRILLA
SERGEANT PEERS
LI (Pronounced "Lee")
A CIVILIAN FLIGHT ANNOUNCER
AN AMERICAN PHOTOGRAPHER
AN AIR FORCE PILOT
AN AMBONESE PSYCHOLOGICAL WARFARE OFFICER
AN AMBONESE SOLDIER

A GUERRILLA INFORMATION OFFICER
OFFICER X
AN AMBONESE NUN

Every sound effect in the play is made, live or on tape, by the EVENT actor. Where possible, the audience should be able to recognize his voice.

# SCENES

# SETTING

A wide, shallow space, as bare of props and set pieces as possible. This will help to characterize the EVENT as the REPORTER sees it: broadly, shallowly, and in sharply isolated fragments.

The back wall should be textured in a range of shades from green to greenish brown, perhaps with collage materials (bamboo, scraps of Asian writing, etc.) blended in. The backdrop must serve alike for city scenes and scenes set in the countryside. To facilitate the EVENT's transformations, masked breaks should be provided in the back wall. Slides announcing the titles of the scenes, etc., appear on the back wall, as do photographs of the EVENT, as described.

# ACT ONE

*As the audience is just about getting settled, the* EVENT *walks into the playing area, stands utterly impassive, and, his mouth moving minimally, begins to articulate a strange and Asian-sounding musical piece. If any stage light is on him, it goes out with the house lights. He continues his instrumental-sounding version of the foreign melody in the darkness.*

Slide: HOW I GOT THAT STORY

Slide: starring

Slide: (ACTOR'S NAME) as THE REPORTER

*(A light comes up as the slide goes off, showing the* RE-PORTER *with pencil poised over his notepad, trying to locate the source of the elusive music. The light goes out.)*

Slide: and

Slide: (ACTOR'S NAME) as THE HISTORICAL EVENT

*(A light comes up on the* EVENT, *from whose passive presence music continues to issue. He is now standing on his head.)*

## Slide: ACCREDITATION

(*Lights come up on the* REPORTER. *He is wearing a rumpled lightweight jacket with ink stains around the pockets. He holds a somewhat crushed felt hat in one hand and speaks to the audience.*)

REPORTER: Hello there. This is Am-bo Land. My new job with the TransPanGlobal Wire Service brought me here. It's not the safest place right now, but this is how I figure it. The last two years I've been reporting on the western part of East Dubuque. A lot goes on there. If you add it all up right, then you've got western East Dubuque. That's fine. But if you add up Am-bo Land, it's every-place. It's *it*. It's what the world is like. If I just keep my eyes wide open I can understand the whole world. That's how I figure it. These are the Am-bo Land offices of TransPanGlobal. Good-sized outfit, hey? I'm here to pick up my accreditation card so I can work incountry. Spell that word without a hyphen.

VOICE: Next. (*The* REPORTER *walks over to a desk. The* DEPUTY COORDINATOR *is sitting behind it.*)

COORDINATOR: May I help you?

REPORTER: I'm here to see Mr. Kingsley.

COORDINATOR: May I ask your business?

REPORTER: I'm just picking up my card so I can work in-country.

COORDINATOR: You'll see Mr. Kingsley.

REPORTER: Thank you.

COORDINATOR: Straight back, third door to the right, first left, and down the hall.

REPORTER: Thanks.

COORDINATOR: He's expecting you.

REPORTER: He is?

COORDINATOR: Yes.

REPORTER: How?

COORDINATOR: You said you work for TransPanGlobal?

REPORTER: Yes.

COORDINATOR: I'm sure you know, then, that our business is communication.

REPORTER: Thank you very much. (*He moves off and into the maze of the* COORDINATOR's *directions. When he gets to* KINGSLEY's *office,* KINGSLEY *is waiting for him. He stands up from his desk and shakes the* REPORTER's *hand.*)

KINGSLEY: I'm so happy to meet you. Please sit down. (*He indicates a chair in front of his desk. The* REPORTER *sits.*) Don't mind if I stare. It's one of the little pleasures of my job when a byline changes to a face. You look quite like your byline, I might say. I couldn't be more pleased.

REPORTER: Well, thank you.

KINGSLEY: I admire your work. Before I'd read two pages of the samples that you sent us, I said, "Bob"—please call me Bob, that's what I call myself—

REPORTER: Okay, Bob.

KINGSLEY: I said, "Bob, this is a man for TransPanGlobal. An impartial man. He views all sides and then he writes the truth as he believes it."

REPORTER: If I may, sir—

KINGSLEY: Bob.

REPORTER: Bob, I'm not sure I'd put it quite that way. I don't think belief is too much help to a reporter. What I try to do is *see*, then write the truth—Bob—as I *see* it.

KINGSLEY: My mistake. Poor choice of words. My meaning was, you don't allow some pietistic preconception to subvert your objectivity. You write what you see.

REPORTER: That's very nicely said, Bob. I'll subscribe to that.

KINGSLEY: On the other hand, you don't write *everything* you see.

REPORTER: I'm not quite sure I—

KINGSLEY: If your wife farts in church you don't run it on the human interest page.

REPORTER: I'm not married.

KINGSLEY: No, I know you're not. That was a figure of speech.

REPORTER: (*"Go on."*) Okay.

KINGSLEY: To bring this down to cases. The Government of Madame Ing is fighting for its life. You probably know that the guerrillas don't confine themselves to Robert's Rules of Order. Madame Ing is forced, in kind, to bite and scratch a little. You may see a few examples. Some abridgement of the freedom of internal opposition. Some abridgement of the outer limbs of those involved. These things may rock you. Nothing wrong with that—as long as you keep one thing very firmly in mind. When we send out reports, the nearest terminal for them is the Imperial Palace. Madame Ing eats ticker tape like eel in fish sauce. That's the A-1 delicacy here, you'll have to try it. Can you handle chopsticks?

REPORTER: Yes, I—

KINGSLEY: Madame Ing is very sensitive to how she's viewed from overseas. Let's face it. When we applied for permission to set up an agency here, we didn't apply to the guerrillas. It's Ing who allowed us to come here, and it's Ing who has the power to send us back. (*Sliding a card across the desk to the* REPORTER.) Let's have a signature.

REPORTER: What's this?

KINGSLEY: Your press card.

REPORTER: (*Pleased.*) Oh. (*He signs.*)

KINGSLEY: (*Deftly seals the card in plastic.*) You'll find this plastic proof against the rainy season, jungle rot—. I took a card like this intact right off the body of a newsman who had all but decomposed.

REPORTER: What happened to him?

KINGSLEY: Madame Ing expelled him but he didn't leave. The will of a developing government will find a way. (*He hands the* REPORTER *his sealed card.*) We're very glad you're with us.
(*Grey-out.* KINGSLEY *disappears as the* REPORTER, *somewhat overloaded, retraces his steps through the maze of* "corridors" *and out onto the streets. His journey is accompanied by the sounds—made on tape, like all the sounds that follow, by the voice of the* EVENT—*of a ticker-tape machine, crossfading with the putt-beep-swish of Hondas.*)

## Slide: TIP

(*Lights full up on the* REPORTER, *still a bit nonplussed as he makes his way along the street. He puts the press card in his hatband and the hat back on his head. The tape ends with a whooshing sound as a sudden wind blows the* REPORTER *to a standstill, makes him grab his hat. He stands quite puzzled.*)

REPORTER: That was odd. A sudden breeze, now nothing. (*He wets his finger and holds it up; shrugs.*) Oriental

weather. (*Starts walking again.*) I've heard that the guerrillas move so fast you feel a wind and don't see anything,
but sitting in your pocket is a bomb. (*A moment's delay,
then frantically he pats his pockets from the chest down.
Gives a sigh of relief. Then, registering something, re-
turns to the first pocket that he checked. Slowly he draws
out a neatly folded sheet of rice paper. Carefully he
opens it. It contains a single wooden match. He reads the
message on the paper.*) "Han Sho Street and Perfume
Boulevard in twenty minutes. A man will ask you for a
light." (*Checking his watch.*) Twenty minutes. That
would be at two o'clock. What time is it now? (*Checking.*) Twenty minutes of two! Excuse me, sir? (*A MAN in
a conical reed hat has walked on.*) Sir. Han Sho Street
and Perfume Boulevard. Which way? (*The MAN snatches
the REPORTER's hat off his head and runs. Chasing him.*)
Hey! Hey! (*A chase ensues, with the MAN appearing
from unexpected places, then vanishing, the REPORTER
farther and farther behind him. A continuation of the
street sounds tape accompanies the chase.*) Hey, come
back here! Stop! I need that! (*Finally the MAN strolls on
with his reed hat in his hand and the REPORTER's on his
head. Puffing, the REPORTER comes in sight.*) Sir, it's not
the hat I want. I won't begrudge you that. I know you
probably live in very straitened circumstances. I just
want the press card. (*The MAN points at an offstage
sign.*) Oh. Han Sho Street and Perfume Boulevard. (*The
MAN holds out his own hat, bottom up. The REPORTER
puts money in it. The MAN takes the REPORTER's hat from
his head and flips it to its owner. Then he ambles off,
counting his money.*) I made it. No one here though. (*He
takes the match out of his pocket and holds it awkwardly
in front of him. After a moment.*) I'll take the opportunity
to absorb a little atmosphere. (*Writing in a little spiral
notebook.*) Busy intersection. People. Hondas. Over there
a big pagoda. Lots of Buddhists in the windows, dressed
in saffron robes. (*As he goes on, the BONZE—in saffron*

*robes—comes on, unseen by him. The* BONZE *is carrying a large red gasoline can.*) All ages. Every window filled with faces. They're all looking over here in my direction. Not at me, though. I don't *think* at me. (*The* BONZE *has "poured" a pool of gasoline on the pavement.*) I can smell their incense. (*The* BONZE *has set the can down and come up behind the* REPORTER. *The* REPORTER *spins around.*) Oh! You startled me. (*Pause. The* BONZE *just stands there.*) Are you my contact? (*Pause.*) You're supposed to ask me something. (*The* BONZE *stands. The* RE- PORTER *starts to hold the match up again, to give the man a hint. The* BONZE *takes it.*) That's not incense! That's gas! (*In one resolute movement, the* BONZE *walks back to the puddle of gas and sits down cross-legged in the middle of it. He "empties" the rest of the can over his head.*)

BONZE: Down with Madame Ing! Down with the repressive government of Am-bo Land! (*He scrapes the match on the pavement and at once is "burning" [a red special and a piece of paper crackled in each hand can give the effect]. The* REPORTER *stands rooted with horror.*)

REPORTER: Oh my god. He's burning. People up and down the street are watching. I am too. I'm watching. (*Quickly.*) I'm not watching. I'm not here! I'm a reporter! I'm recording this! (*He writes.*) "The monk was sitting in the center of a column of fire. From time to time a light wind blew the flames away from his face. His face was twisted with the pain." The pain, my god—! (*To himself.*) No! You're not here. You're just recording this. You look at it, you take the pencil, and you write it down. (*The* BONZE *topples sideways.*) My god. (*He forces his pencil to his pad and writes. Tape fades up: a low repeating chant in an Asian-sounding language.*) ". . . Charred black . . . black circle on the pavement . . . wisps of orange fabric drifted down the street . . ." (*The lights fade out. The chant continues in the darkness.*)

Slide: AUDIENCE

(*Lights come up on the* REPORTER, *still shaken from his experience at the street corner.*)

REPORTER: I went and talked this morning to the Reverend Father of the Han Sho Street Pagoda. Here. (*He takes out his notebook.*) I think I've got it clear now. He explained to me that the—what's that? (*He can't read his writing.*)—the immolation was a political act and a spiritual act at the same time. There are six thousand monks in Am-bo Land. Of these six thousand, one hundred and fifty have applied for permission to kill themselves. They wish to demonstrate their faith. But the Reverend Father withholds permission till the worldly motive—political protest—is sufficient by itself to justify the act. (*Quoting.*) "The spiritual act must be politically pure; the political act must be spiritually pure." It's both at once. And so it's sort of—neither . . . If I'd had some sand or water— or I might have tried to damp the fire with my jacket— but that would have been unethical . . . I've got it all down here, though. (*A gong sounds. The* REPORTER *starts.*) The most amazing thing has happened! I'm about to talk to Madame Ing! She summoned me! Reporters have waited years without getting an audience. I can't believe this is happening. (*The gong sounds again, a little louder. The* REPORTER *walks awestruck into the Presence.* MADAME ING *is seated, regally.*)

ING: Here I sit and stand.

REPORTER: Um . . . yes. (*At a loss what to say.*) I've seen you on the cover of *Time* magazine.

ING: Do not mention that loathsome publication in my presence.

REPORTER: But they named you "Woman of the Year."

ING: What year?

REPORTER: Why, last year.

ING: Why not this year?

REPORTER: They never give it to anyone twice in a row.

ING: In my country one must grow in honor as one grows in years. *Time* should have named me "Woman of the Decade," next year "Woman of the Century," and so on. I have summoned you.

REPORTER: I'm flabbergasted.

ING: I wish not to know what that word means.

REPORTER: To what do I owe the extraordinary honor of your summons?

ING: To your crime.

REPORTER: My crime?

ING: You bribed the monks of Han Sho Street Pagoda to set one of their fellows on fire.

REPORTER: What?

ING: They filled his veins with morphine till his blood was thin. They led him to the street and they set fire to him.

REPORTER: That's not true.

ING: Not true?

REPORTER: No. The man was alone. Nobody led him to the street.

ING: Then he was hypnotized.

REPORTER: He wasn't.

ING: How do you know?

REPORTER: Because I heard him speak.

ING: A man can speak under hypnosis.

REPORTER: Well, I'm sure he wasn't hypnotized.

ING: Men of the press are expected to have documentation for what they say. Do you have proof?

REPORTER: I saw him.

ING: Look at me. You see my face?

REPORTER: Yes . . .

ING: Am I smiling?

REPORTER: (*Peering as through darkness at her unreadable expression.*) I don't know.

ING: The monk was hypnotized.

REPORTER: *You* have no proof.

ING: I know. You have admitted you do not know. Madame Ing has won that argument.

REPORTER: All right, then, let's just say that he was hypnotized. What makes you think I was behind it?

ING: I have proof.

REPORTER: What proof?

ING: Sheer logic. Highly valued in the West. Tell me what reason might this monk have had to light himself on fire?

REPORTER: Well, I've done a little work on that. His motives were political, exclusively—and therefore they were purely of the spirit. Only by being entirely the one and not at all the other could they be entirely the other and I really thought I had that.

ING: On his first day in my country, a reporter puts this barbecue on ticker tapes that go to every land. Is this not good for his career?

REPORTER: No—!

ING: No?

REPORTER: Well, yes—

ING: You are the one man with a motive for this foolishness.

REPORTER: I didn't do it.

ING: You have proof?

REPORTER: No—.

ING: I have shown you *my* proof. Madame Ing has won *that* argument. It is time to do my dance for you. (*She breaks toward a standing screen.*)

REPORTER: Madame Ing, I hope you won't expel me.

ING: No. You may be wrong.

REPORTER: Wrong?

ING: You may *not* have bribed the monks to burn their friend. (*The gong sounds.* MADAME ING *passes behind the screen; emerges draped in a flowing costume.*) I have an army and I have a private army. (*Dancing a prelude.*) My private army is made up entirely of women.

REPORTER: Yes, I know.

ING: (*Silencing him.*) I speak to speak. I do not speak to give you information. Objections have been raised because I pay my women more than my regular army. But my women are all officers, down to the lowest private. Now I present the guerrilla chief. (*She assumes the posture of a bent-haunched, quavering man.*) And this is the lowest of my Paramilitary Girls. (*She strikes the stance of a tall, fierce woman. In the dance that follows—a solo version of the entire Peking Opera—the Paramilitary Girl fights with the guerrilla and defeats him.* ING *withdraws behind her screen. Unseen, she uses a device to alter her* *voice—say, a $10 can. Reverberant.*) You find us inscrutable here in the East.

REPORTER: It's not just you. It's the Americans here too. I can't—

ING: Be patient. Soon you will understand even less. Your ignorance will be whipped with wind until it is pure as mist above the mountains. But you must await this time with patience—patient as the rocks. We will never be perfectly inscrutable to you till we have killed you and you do not know why. (*The gong sounds.*)

REPORTER: Does that mean I go now? (*Silence. The RE-PORTER starts off as the lights fade out. Slides: on the back wall appear glimpses of parts of the face of the actor playing the EVENT. Each slide shows just a single feature. The slides are in exaggerated half-tone—broken into dots as if for reproduction—and thus suggestive of pictures in a newspaper. If the slides come from more than one projector, they should alternate arrhythmically.*)

## Slide: STRIP

(*The REPORTER is standing on the sidewalk of the Strip.*)

REPORTER: These people in power are a little hard to fathom. So I've come here, to the street they call the Strip. This is where the real people come, the normal, regular people. And what better place to look for the reality of this moment in history? Who better to talk to than the G.I.'s and the Government troops, the bar girls and the peddlers, people trying just to get along, to live their lives, to snatch a moment of pleasure or excitement in the midst of the horror and confusion of this war? (*He starts to walk.*) The bars have names like China Doll, Las Vegas, there's the Dragon Bar, that one's the Playboy. Up

and down the street are skinny men in short sleeves
selling local soda dyed bright red and blue. Little bare-
foot boys are selling dirty pictures. That is, I'm sure
they're dirty. I assume they're dirty. Filthy, probably. (*A*
Boy *has pattered on. He thrusts three or four pictures at
the* Reporter, *arrayed like playing cards.*) No thank you,
I don't want to see them. No, but wait a minute. I should
look. They're part of local color. (*He pays the* Boy *and
takes the pictures. Quickly joking to the audience.*)
Nope, they're black-and-white. (*Back to the pictures.*)
That's awful. Would you look at that? That's terrible.
(*Putting the pictures in his pocket.*) These are docu-
ments. These say it all. (*A* G.I. *passes the* Reporter. *He
is looking very wired.*) There's a G.I. going into that bar.
I'm going to interview him. (*Reading the sign above the
"door" the* G.I. *has gone through.*) "Mimi's Flamboyant."
Here I go—(*He chokes off, coughing, fans the smoke
away from his face. There is a blast of instrumental music
—a tinny imitation of Western rock-and-roll, say, "Satis-
faction."*) * The music's so loud I can hardly see the people's faces. Where did my G.I. go? It's dark in here but
all the girls are wearing sunglasses. The girls look very
young. They're pretty. No, that's not objective. Stick to
what's objective. But they are. (*The* G.I. *comes in from
the back, carrying a drink. He looks spent. He sits down
at a table.*) Look, there's my G.I. now. Excuse me, soldier, can I talk to you?

G.I.: (*Looks at him stonily.*) About what?

REPORTER: All this.

G.I.: All what?

REPORTER: The whole thing.

G.I.: You in the army?

REPORTER: No.

* See special note on copyright page.

ING: We will never be perfectly inscrutable to you until we have
killed you and you do not know why.

G.I.: You in the army?
REPORTER: No.
G.I.: Then what in the fuck are you doin over here?

REPORTER: What happened to your arm?
PHOTOGRAPHER: Ooh that was righteous. It was night time. I was standing
getting pictures of the tracer patterns. BAMMO! from behind! I got an
incredible shot of that arm flying off. WHOOSH! Little bit underexposed,
but something else, man. WHOOSH!

GUERRILLA: You worked within the system of our enemies and subject to their interests.

REPORTER: Partly subject.

GUERRILLA: Yet you say that you have never done us any harm.

REPORTER: All I found out as a reporter was I'd never find out anything.

GUERRILLA: Do we pardon an enemy sniper if his marksmanship is poor?

© 1982 GERRY GOODSTEIN

G.I.: Then what in the fuck are you doin over here?

REPORTER: It's my beat. I'm a reporter.

G.I.: A reporter? All right. Ask your questions.

REPORTER: What's it like?

G.I.: What's what like?

REPORTER: Combat.

G.I.: Scary.

REPORTER: Scary?

G.I.: What the fuck you think?

REPORTER: I figured it was scary.

G.I.: You're a fuckin genius. Ask some more.

REPORTER: I don't think we've exhausted that subject yet.

G.I.: Naw, you got it figured, man. It's scary. You got that one fuckin *down*.

REPORTER: Tell me some stories.

G.I.: Stories?

REPORTER: Anecdotes. Some things that happened.

G.I.: Only one thing happens, baby. You're out there in the jungle, right? The fuckin boonies. Everything is green. And then the bullet comes. Your name is on it. That's the story.

REPORTER: Your name is on it?

G.I.: That's a rodge.

REPORTER: What if your name's not on it?

G.I.: Then it misses you and hits your buddy.

REPORTER: Do you have to duck?

G.I.: What?

REPORTER: Do you duck?

G.I.: Your mama drop you on your head when you was little?

REPORTER: So you duck then?

G.I.: Man, you hug that ground like it was Raquel fuckin Welch.

REPORTER: But if the bullet hasn't got your name, it isn't going to hit you.

G.I.: Right.

REPORTER: And if it's got your name—

G.I.: Man, if it's got your name, you can dig a hole and roll an APC on top of you, don't make no never mind.

REPORTER: Then why do you duck?

G.I.: Someone's shooting at your ass, you duck!

REPORTER: It still seems like a contradiction. Guess you've got to go out there and see it for yourself.

G.I.: Out where?

REPORTER: The boonies.

G.I.: Are you batshit?

REPORTER: Huh?

G.I.: You're going out there?

REPORTER: Yeah.

G.I.: What for?

REPORTER: I want to see. (*Showing his notebook.*) I've got a job to do.

G.I.: You want to see. Tomorrow morning you wake up in your hotel room, you say, fine day, think I'll grab a chopper, go on out and hump the boonies. That ain't it, man. You can't want to go. Somebody got to make you go. Some mean old sergeant, damnfool captain got to tell you, soldier, grab your gear and get your ass out there and hump. You can't want to go.

REPORTER: I won't get out there if it's not by choice. I have to want to.

G.I.: I'm gonna tell you something, hombre. I'm gonna tell you once, so listen. You go out there if you're gonna, but you don't come near my unit. Do you read me? We get hit for sure. You're *bad luck*. You come close to my platoon, I'm gonna waste your ass. You'll never know what hit you. (*Exiting into the back.*) Mama! Mamasan! Hey mama!
(*Blackout. Tape: the sound of helicopters in flight, then setting down—without, however, turning off their rotors.*)


Slide: FIELD


(*The* REPORTER *in the field. He has put a mottled green flak jacket over his shirt, and is wearing a tiger-fatigue hat with his accreditation card tucked in the camouflage band. He speaks into the microphone of a cassette recorder that hangs off his hip.*)

REPORTER: This is your correspondent in Am-bo Land, reporting from the field. I've gone out with an American reconnaissance platoon. The choppers dropped us in a clearing. We've regrouped behind the treeline. (*Lights up on* LIEUTENANT THIBODEAUX, *speaking to the troops.*)

LIEUTENANT: Sweet Jesus fuckin string my balls and hang me from a fuckin tree, Christ fuckin motherfuck god damn! Because this war has taught me two things, men. It's taught me how to kill and it's taught me how to swear. God fuckin crap-eye son of a bee, and cunt my fuckin jungle rot and hang me fuckin upside-down and jangle my cojones. Joy roll! Fuckin-A! You hear me, men?

REPORTER: That's Lieutenant Thibodeaux. He's trying to help his troops achieve the right aggressive attitude.

LIEUTENANT: You hear me, men?

SOLDIERS: (*On tape; with no trace of enthusiasm.*) Yeah.

LIEUTENANT: Sound off like you got a pair! We're Airborne! Say it!

SOLDIERS: Airborne.

LIEUTENANT: Well, that's not outstanding, but it's better. Slip my disc and tie my tubes, god damn and fuckin motherfuck!

REPORTER: He has to win the absolute confidence of the men in his command. If he's not able to, in combat, when he's giving them an order that requires them to risk their lives, it's possible that one of them may shoot him in the back. The soldiers call this "fragging."

LIEUTENANT: I won't lie to you. This is a dangerous mission. But I want you to know, men, I've been out there and I've come back. I've come back every god damn time. That's every motherloving asslick shitbrick pick your nose and fuck me time. I don't wear decorations in the field, but if any man here doesn't believe me he can come to my hootch when this thing is over and I'll show him my Sharpshooter's Badge with four bars and my two Good Conduct Medals. Suck my dick and kick my ass six ways from Sunday. Sing it with me.
I wanna be an Airborne Ranger
I wanna be an Airborne Ranger
I wanna lead a life of danger.

SOLDIERS: (*Barely audible.*) I wanna lead a life of danger.

LIEUTENANT: 'Cause I fight out there beside my men. And

here's one thing I promise you. If I give any of you men an order that requires you to lay down your life, it's because I'm wearing army green. I love this uniform. I love the army. Good luck, men. Let's move out! (*He turns and takes a step away. A shot rings out.* THIBODEAUX's *limbs sprawl outwards as the lights black out. Almost immediately, the lights pick up the* REPORTER *in the same spot where he stood at the beginning of the scene. Once more, he speaks into his tape recorder.*)

REPORTER: This is your correspondent in Am-bo Land, reporting from the field. Our mission was almost aborted by a circumstance the facts aren't quite all in on yet. We'll proceed with Sergeant Peers in charge. He's forming the platoon into a line. I'm supposed to walk at the end. The men say that'll give me the best view of everything that happens. (*He walks in a circle, falling in behind the last soldier*—PFC PROCHASKA. PROCHASKA *carries an M-16 rifle. They hump the boonies during the following, the* REPORTER *carefully copying everything* PROCHASKA *does.*) Excuse me? Soldier?

PFC: (*Turning.*) Yeah? Hey, stagger!

REPORTER: Stagger?

PFC: Don't walk in a line with me! Some sniper hits you gets me too.

REPORTER: (*Sidestepping.*) Check. Soldier?

PFC: Don't call me soldier. I got drafted. Call me Prochaska.

REPORTER: Check.

PFC: And keep it down.

REPORTER: (*More quietly.*) Is this your first patrol?

PFC: Do pigs shit ice cream?

REPORTER: (*Not understanding.*) No . . . (*Speaking fur-*

*tively into his cassette recorder.*) "Do pigs shit ice cream?" Look that up. (*To* Prochaska.) What's the purpose—the objective—of this patrol?

PFC: Find the enemy.

REPORTER: Do you expect it to succeed?

PFC: I hope not.

REPORTER: Are you afraid?

PFC: Do cows have titties?

REPORTER: Yes . . . (*Into his recorder.*) Check "Do cows have titties?" (*To* Prochaska.) You don't think I'm bad luck, do you?

PFC: No, you good luck, brother.

REPORTER: Good luck? Super. Although it would defeat my entire purpose to affect the outcome of the mission in any way. But why am I good luck?

PFC: You're walking behind me.

REPORTER: Huh?

PFC: Go-rillas spring an ambush, the man in the back gets shot first.

REPORTER: Sure. That stands to reason.

PFC: You're not carrying a rifle either. They gonna take you for a medic.

REPORTER: What does that mean?

PFC: First they shoot the officer. Then they shoot the medic.

REPORTER: I thought they shot the man in back first.

PFC: Brother, either way . . .

REPORTER: I want to get this straight. Let's say for now that I'm not here, so you're the man in back. Good. Now the officer is Sergeant Peers, and there's the medic. Okay. So, the man in back and the officer get shot before the medic. But which of you gets shot first?

PFC: Man, we all get shot if you keep talking.

REPORTER: The sergeant is raising his hand. What does that mean?

PFC: Break time. You smoke?

REPORTER: No.

PFC: Save me your ciggies from your C's, okay?

REPORTER: Sure.

PFC: Don't sit near the radio. You do, they shoot you first. (*He walks off. The* REPORTER *sits in place.*)

REPORTER: When PFC Prochaska said "C's," his reference was to C-rations, the G.I.'s meal-in-a-box. I'm about to open my first box of C's. (*He takes a small box out of his pack. Reading.*) "Meal, Combat, Individual." (*He opens the box and finds a paper napkin on top; tucks it into his shirt like a bib. Then he goes through the assorted tins and packets, reading their printed contents.*) Cigarettes. (*He puts the little four-pack of cigarettes aside for* PROCHASKA.) Beans with Frankfurter Chunks in Tomato Sauce. Towel, Paper, Cleansing, Wet, Antiseptic. Inter-dental Stimulator. Cream substitute, Dry, Non-dairy. Chiclets. (*He takes out a book of matches with an olive-drab cover.*) "These matches are designed especially for damp climates. They will not light when wet." (*While the* REPORTER *has been busy with his C's, a* GUERRILLA *has appeared behind him, wearing foliage for camou-flage. He has watched the* REPORTER *for a moment, in-humanly still; then, with very small gestures to right and left, has closed in his fellow guerrillas—who are unseen—around the Americans for an ambush, and has vanished. Now the* REPORTER *fingers a small white wad.*)

Toilet paper. (*The ambush is sprung. The* REPORTER *holds up his accreditation card. The firing is deafening, intolerably loud. It continues longer than its intensity would seem to allow, then quite suddenly it stops completely; all at once explodes again. The* REPORTER *low-crawls frantically away, nearly running into* SERGEANT PEERS, *who, having reached low ground, starts tuning in the field phone he is carrying. It has a receiver like a regular telephone, leaving one of the* SERGEANT's *ears free.*)

SERGEANT: (*To the* REPORTER.) Cover my back.

REPORTER: What? Sergeant Peers, it's—(*He was going to say "me."*)

SERGEANT: All behind my back's your field of fire.

REPORTER: I haven't got a weapon.

SERGEANT: (*Looking at him for the first time.*) Christ, it's that one. (*He goes back to the radio.*)

REPORTER: What happens now?

SERGEANT: I try and get my god damn channel.

REPORTER: Where's the radio man?

SERGEANT: Which piece of him?

REPORTER: (*Taking out his notebook.*) What was his name?

SERGEANT: (*Into the radio.*) HQ!

REPORTER: Was he a draftee or did he enlist?

SERGEANT: At ease, god damn it!

REPORTER: Sarge, I've got to get some facts. If I'm not getting facts there isn't any purpose to my being here.

SERGEANT: HQ!

REPORTER: I mean, consider for a moment what my situation is. I don't know anything I didn't know before I got here. What if I get killed? I don't know why that monk was burning, what my boss wants—. What's the word for this? Condition Red?

SERGEANT: (*Into the phone.*) HQ! We're pinned down. Our coordinates are 5730 by 9324.

REPORTER: What's your serial number?

SERGEANT: Will you shut the fuck up?

REPORTER: I'm not getting any news! If I'm not getting any news then what in Christ's name am I doing here? (*A grenade bursts. The* REPORTER *is hit in the rump.*) I'm hit.

SERGEANT: Don't move. (*He quickly checks the wound.*) You're all right.

REPORTER: No I'm not all right. I'm hit.

SERGEANT: You're okay.

REPORTER: Is there blood?

SERGEANT: No sweat. You're gonna see that girl. (*Handing him a pressure dressing.*) Here. Hold this on the wound.

REPORTER: It hurts! I'm going to die! They're going to kill me! Get me out of here! Christ Jesus, get me out of here! (*A whistling.*)

SERGEANT: Here comes the artillery! Flatten!
(*With the* SERGEANT'S *last word there comes a blackout, then a monstrous crashing, ten times louder than before. The barrage continues in the darkness.*)

## Slide: IMPRINTMENT

(*Lights come up on the* REPORTER *in a hospital bed. He is sleeping. There is a little cabinet next to the bed, with a phone on it. The* REPORTER'S *field clothes are folded on a shelf underneath. His cassette recorder is on top. A knock comes at the door—a very soft one. The* REPORTER *doesn't register it, but he stirs, rearranges himself for more sleep—sees the audience.*)

REPORTER: Where am I? (*He sits partway up and feels a rush of pain.*) Ow! Excuse me. (*Discreetly, he lifts the sheet and turns his hip; remembers.*) Oh yeah. What day is this? The last thing I remember is the medic and the morphine. I should find out where I am. (*He makes a move to get up; stops mid-motion.*) I feel dizzy. (*The soft knock is repeated.*) Come in? (Li *enters: a small, pretty Ambonese bar girl. She walks with little steps into the room.*) Hello.

LI: You sleep?

REPORTER: No, I'm awake. Are you the nurse?

LI: My name Li. Bar girl. I work Coral Bar. You know?

REPORTER: Um—no, I've never been there.

LI: I come here too. Man downstairs who sometime let me in. Are you G.I.?

REPORTER: No.

LI: See? I know you not G.I. I like you better than G.I. (*Coming further into the room.*) You very nice.

REPORTER: (*Holding her off.*) No, I'm not nice. I'm a reporter.

LI: Li not understand.

REPORTER: I'm someone who's not here—who's here but can't—do anything, except report.

LI: (*Puzzled.*) You like I go away?

REPORTER: No, you don't have to go away . . .

LI: You lonely.

REPORTER: No I'm not. Not *lonely* . . .

LI: Yes, you lonely. I see.

REPORTER: I'm *alone*. It's a condition of the job.

LI: You tired.

REPORTER: Well, they've given me some medication . . .

LI: You lie down.

REPORTER: I'm lying down.

LI: You lie down all the way—

REPORTER: (*Escapes by jumping out of bed—he is wearing blue institutional pyjamas.*) I've got a wonderful idea.

LI: No, where you go?

REPORTER: You sit down. Sit down on the bed. (*Going into the pockets of his field clothes.*) Look, here's some money for your time. There's fifty *hoi*. Is that enough? I'm going to interview you.

LI: (*Not knowing the word.*) In-ter-view?
(*The* REPORTER *has laid two small colored bills on the bed. Li picks them up and, somewhat uncertainly, sits down on the bed. The* REPORTER *sets up his tape recorder.*)

REPORTER: I've been feeling, lately, quite confused. I think that maybe, if I just can try and understand one person who's involved in all this, then I might be onto something. Will you tell me your story?

LI: Oh, you like me tell you *story*. Now I see. I have G.I. friend teach me tell him your Jack and the Beanstalk. When I get to part where beanstalk grow I stop and he say "Fee Fi Fo Fum"—

REPORTER: Not that kind of story. Just your life. Where do you come from?

LI: Where you like I come from?

REPORTER: From wherever you were born.

LI: Okay. I try. (*Thinks a second, sizing the* REPORTER *up.*) I was born in little village. I hate the guerrillas. Was so glad when many helicopters come all full of big Americans. Americans with big guns. You have gun?

REPORTER: No.

LI: Yes you do. I know you have gun.

REPORTER: No, I don't.

LI: Yes, great big huge big gun and shoot so straight—

REPORTER: (*Turns off the tape.*) No, no. That isn't what I want, Li. I just want your story. Nothing else.

LI: You shy.

REPORTER: It's just a question of professional procedure.

LI: You like woman to be like a man. I see now. Now I tell my story.

REPORTER: Wait. (*He switches on his tape.*) Go.

LI: I am spy. My name not Li at all.

REPORTER: What is it?

LI: My name *Gad Da Lai I Rang Toi Doung*. That mean Woman Who Love to Watch Foreigners Die. I hate Americans.

REPORTER: Now we're getting down to cases. I'll bet all you girls hate Americans.

LI: (*Encouraged.*) Yes. I love to kill them.

REPORTER: Have you killed very many?

LI: Every day I kill one or I no can sleep. I like to pull their veins out with my little white sharp teeth. This is only thing can make Li happy with a man.

REPORTER: (*Getting drawn in.*) Wow. That's *political.*

LI: I like to climb on top of you and bite you, chew your neck until your bones are in my teeth and then I crack them—

REPORTER: Stop! You're making this up too. Li, don't you understand? I want your real story. (LI *has found the light switch on the wall above the bed and turned it off.*) Li, turn the lights back on.

LI: You tired.

REPORTER: I'm not tired, I just *feel* tired.

LI: You come here.

REPORTER: I'll bring the tape recorder and we'll talk some more.

LI: You like it in my country?

REPORTER: (*Sitting on the bed.*) No. I hate it. I don't understand what anybody's doing. I don't like it here at all.

LI: You like I turn lights on?

REPORTER: Yes.

LI: There. (*The lights are still off.*)

REPORTER: There what?

LI: You no see lights? Then you have eyes closed.

REPORTER: No—

LI: I turn lights off again. (*She leaves them off.*) You like that?

REPORTER: Are they on or off?

LI: You lie down.

REPORTER: (*Does.*) Do you wear sunglasses indoors? At Mimi's all the girls wear very dark dark glasses. Are you touching me? You're not supposed to touch me.

LI: I no touch you. (*She is touching him.*)

REPORTER: I saw a man burn with a lot of people watching. I saw Ing dance. I was in the jungle and a piece of flying metal flew so fast you couldn't see it but it stopped inside my body. I'm in Am-bo Land. (*The phone rings.*) The phone? (*He picks it up.*) Hello? (*Pause.*) Mr. Kingsley, yes, hello! (*Pause.*) You're here? Wait just a little second, Mr. Kingsley. (*Turning the lights on.*) Li? (*She is gone. The* REPORTER *looks puzzled but relieved. He takes the phone back up—interrupts his movement to make a quick check under the bed, but* LI *is truly gone. Into the phone.*) I'm sorry, sir—Hello? (*KINGSLEY bursts in, bearing flowers.*)

KINGSLEY: Hey there, how's the Purple Heart?

REPORTER: Hello, sir—

KINGSLEY: (*Points a mock-stern finger at him.*) Sir?

REPORTER: Bob! Hello, Bob. You're so thoughtful to come visit me.

KINGSLEY: (*Seeing the cassette recorder, which is still in the* REPORTER's *lap.*) I see you made a tape. You gonna pay the girl residuals? (*The* REPORTER *looks at the machine, then turns it off.*) I got here half an hour ago and saw her coming in here. Figured this'd give you time enough. Hell, just in from the field most guys don't need but twenty seconds. (*He plunks down the flowers on the cabinet.*)

REPORTER: I was interviewing her.

KINGSLEY: Here's something else you'll need. (*He takes a red-white-and-blue card out of his vest pocket and hands it to the* REPORTER.)

REPORTER: What's this?

KINGSLEY: A business card.

REPORTER: (*Looks at it.*) It's just a number.

KINGSLEY: You hold onto that.

REPORTER: (*Slips it in his shirt pocket.*) Who is it?

KINGSLEY: Officer X.

REPORTER: Who's that?

KINGSLEY: He's probably lots of people. First-rate resource. He's got access to army supply lines. Got a couple of straws in the Ambonese milkshake too. You'll want a stereo system for starters. And an ice machine.

REPORTER: I don't need—

KINGSLEY: It's all on TransPanGlobal. X already has your name. Hey, you're our boy! We wouldn't want you cooped up here without a few amenities.

REPORTER: I've only got a flesh wound. I'll be out of here tomorrow, or today.

KINGSLEY: Today. Tomorrow.

REPORTER: Next day at the latest.

KINGSLEY: I guess you know you got off pretty easy.

REPORTER: Yes, I guess I did.

KINGSLEY: Good luck, huh?

REPORTER: Guess it was.

KINGSLEY: Good luck for you. Bad luck for TransPanGlobal.

REPORTER: How?

KINGSLEY: This thing has hit us right smack in the middle of a gore gap.

REPORTER: Gore gap?

KINGSLEY: Little guy from *Aujourd'hui* lost his esophagus

last week. Two weeks ago some wop from *Benvenuto* got
his ear blown off. We haven't had an injury for five
months. God damn outlets don't believe you're really covering a war unless some blood flows with the ink. So let's
say we announce your little contretemps the way it really
happened. "On such-and-such a day our correspondent
sallied forth to get the news. In the performance of his
duty, he was wounded." (*As a questioner.*) "Where?"
"He took a little shrapnel." "Where?" "He took a little
shrapnel in the ass." (*To the* REPORTER.) Not too impres-
sive. Let me ask you something. Why should we accept
that you were wounded where you were and let the
whole of TransPanGlobal look like shitheads—are you
with me?—when a half a foot—six inches—from your per-
forated fanny is your spine?

REPORTER: My spine?

KINGSLEY: We're going to say the shrapnel lodged against
your lower vertebrae. That's nothing that a brilliant sur-
geon, luck, and a short convalescence can't cure.

REPORTER: How short?

KINGSLEY: Three months.

REPORTER: Three months?

KINGSLEY: The spine's a very tricky area.

REPORTER: Why do you assume I'll go along with this?

KINGSLEY: We brought you here.

REPORTER: You brought me where?

KINGSLEY: To Am-bo Land.

REPORTER: That's supposed to make me grateful?

KINGSLEY: Don't you like it here?

REPORTER: What makes you even possibly imagine that I
like it here?

KINGSLEY: By this point in their tour, we've found that most reporters have experienced imprintment.

REPORTER: What's—

KINGSLEY: Imprintment. A reporter goes to cover a country and the country covers him.

REPORTER: You think that Am-bo Land is covering me?

KINGSLEY: It's just a guess.

REPORTER: A guess.

KINGSLEY: That's all.

REPORTER: All right. I'm going to show you just how good a guess it is. (*He gets out of bed.*)

KINGSLEY: What are you doing?

REPORTER: (*Getting his clothes out of the cabinet.*) You see these socks? They're decomposing with the climate. Not the rain and mud. The *air.* The air is putrid in this country. When I go to put on clean socks in the morning they all smell as if some stranger took and *wore* them in the night. (*He flings the socks away and starts to pull on his field clothes over his pyjamas.*) I can't *believe* you thought that Am-bo Land was covering me. It's true that I can't do my job, if that's the same thing. I can never tell what's going on. Nobody ever gives me any answers. If they do I'm asking stupid questions. That's not how my life is supposed to go! I won't accept that! I refuse! It doesn't rain here when it rains. It sweats. The palm leaves drip sweat even in the sunshine. Have you tried the beer? It's great. Tastes like the inside of a monkey's armpits.

KINGSLEY: Where are you going?

REPORTER: First I'm going to the airbase. That's four miles. From there, eleven thousand miles to East Dubuque.

KINGSLEY: You're leaving?

REPORTER: That's eleven thousand-four miles. I'll be counting every centimeter.

KINGSLEY: What about the gore gap?

REPORTER: Blow your brains out. That'll fill it.

KINGSLEY: This is highly unprofessional. You know that.

REPORTER: No I don't. I don't know anything. I only know I'm going.

KINGSLEY: If you're going, I won't try to stop you.

REPORTER: Great. Goodbye. (*Limping slightly, he starts out.*)

KINGSLEY: You're sure you want to go?

REPORTER: I'm sure!

KINGSLEY: Enjoy your flight.

REPORTER: You bet I will! I'll savor every second! (*He slams out. Blackout. Tape:* A CIVILIAN FLIGHT ANNOUNCER *speaks over an outdoor loudspeaker.*)

FLIGHT ANNOUNCER: (*In a voice that reeks routine.*) Attention on the runway please . . . Attention on the runway please . . . Lone Star Airlines Flight 717 has completed its boarding procedure . . . Clear the runway please . . . Please clear the runway . . . No more passengers may board at this time . . . (*With a little more urgency.*) Will the gentleman please clear the runway . . . Flight 717 is taking off . . . The gentleman is standing in the backblast . . . Will the gentleman please limp a little faster, he is about to be cremated . . .

Slide: PLANES

(*Simultaneously with the slide, the* REPORTER *shouts from offstage.*)

REPORTER: (*Live.*) Okay! Okay! (*Lights up on a black-and-yellow barrier with the legend,* "Do Not Pass Beyond This Point.")

FLIGHT ANNOUNCER: (*Still on tape.*) Will the gimp in the pyjama top accelerate his pace please . . .

REPORTER: (*Still offstage, but closer.*) Yes, *o-kay!*

FLIGHT ANNOUNCER: Now will the moron kindly haul his ass behind the yellow barrier and await the next plane out at that location.

REPORTER: (*Rushing on in total disarray.*) Yes, all *right!* I'm here! I'm *here!*
(*He crawls under the barrier, ending up on the downstage side. The* PHOTOGRAPHER *hobbles on from the opposite direction. He is missing an arm. One foot is in a huge cast. His clothes are multi-layered and multi-colored, and include a Clint Eastwood-style serape. Sundry cameras, lens cases, filter cases hang from straps around his neck and shoulders. A sign on his floppy field hat reads,* "Say Cheese.")

PHOTOGRAPHER: Hey man, I need a little help with something, can you help me out?

REPORTER: (*Just sits on the asphalt, panting.*) Damn it! *Damn* it!

PHOTOGRAPHER: Missed your plane, huh? That's a drag.

REPORTER: There's not another plane for seven hours.

PHOTOGRAPHER: There's one in fifteen minutes. That's the help I need.

REPORTER: (*Pulls himself up by the barrier.*) In fifteen minutes? Where?

PHOTOGRAPHER: (*Pointing offstage.*) Right over there. The Weasel. See? She's sleeping. But in fifteen minutes she'll be up there in the sky. It fucks your mind up.

REPORTER: That's a bomber.

PHOTOGRAPHER: Dig it.

REPORTER: I need a passenger plane.

PHOTOGRAPHER: (*Enlightened.*) You mean a plane to *go* somewhere. Okay, man. Not too zen, but—. Wanna help me out?

REPORTER: If I can.

PHOTOGRAPHER: (*Extends his foot cast to be pulled off like a boot.*) Here. Help me ditch this plaster, willya?

REPORTER: What's it on for?

PHOTOGRAPHER: German paper that I sometimes sell my snaps to wanted pictures of a minefield. Who knows why, right? Only, dig it man, the thing about a minefield is it looks like any other field. I mean like that's the whole idea, right? So I tramped a lot of paddies before I found one. Got an action shot, though. KRUUMP!

REPORTER: What happened to your arm?

PHOTOGRAPHER: Ooh that was righteous. It was night time. I was standing getting pictures of the tracer patterns. BAMMO! from behind! I got an incredible shot of that arm flying off. WHOOSH! Little bit underexposed, but something else, man. WHOOSH!

REPORTER: I think you ought to take my flight with me.

PHOTOGRAPHER: You wouldn't wanna leave if you could make these bomb runs.

REPORTER: I could make the bomb runs.

PHOTOGRAPHER: Nix. They just give seats to newsmen.

REPORTER: I'm a reporter.

PHOTOGRAPHER: Yeah? Well shit man, what you waiting for? Come help me get my foot up in the cockpit and then climb on in yourself.

REPORTER: No way. I've got a plane to catch.

PHOTOGRAPHER: These babies drop their goodies and they come right back. Takes half an hour.

REPORTER: They come back in half an hour?

PHOTOGRAPHER: Like a boomerang. Come on.

REPORTER: Not me.

PHOTOGRAPHER: I'm telling you, these flights are ab-*stract*.

REPORTER: Even if I wanted to, I couldn't.

PHOTOGRAPHER: Why not?

REPORTER: 'Cause they wouldn't let me on.

PHOTOGRAPHER: You're a reporter.

REPORTER: No I'm not. I was. I quit.

PHOTOGRAPHER: You quit?

REPORTER: That's right.

PHOTOGRAPHER: You give your card back?

REPORTER: (*Lies.*)—Yes.

PHOTOGRAPHER: You didn't, man. It's right there on your hat.

REPORTER: (*Taking it out of the hatband.*) I still have the card.

PHOTOGRAPHER: Come on! We're gonna miss the takeoff! It's outrageous, man, it pulls your smile till it's all the way back of your head! (*He disappears.*)

REPORTER: (*Calling after him.*) I'm not going to go. I'll help you load your cast in, but I'm not going to go.

PHOTOGRAPHER: (*Off.*) Come *on*, man!

REPORTER: Okay, but I'm only going to help you with your cast . . .

(*He follows the* PHOTOGRAPHER *off. Blackout. Tape: an orientation by the* AIR FORCE PILOT, *crackling as if over earphones in a helmet.*)

PILOT: I'm gonna tell you right off I don't want you here. I don't know why they let reporters on bomb runs and I'm damned if I'm gonna worry about you. This is a vertical mission. If they hit us while we're diving, I'll try to get the plane in a horizontal position, then I'll jump.

### Slide: RUN

PILOT: That means there won't be any pilot, so you'll probably want to jump too. (*Lights come up on the* RE-PORTER *and the* PHOTOGRAPHER *seated in the plane. They are both wearing helmets. As the* PILOT *continues, the* REPORTER *tries to locate the devices he mentions.*) There are two handles beside your seat. Move the one on the right first down then up. Your seat will eject you and your chute will open automatically. If the chute doesn't open you've got a spare, pull the cord on the front of your flight jacket. If that chute doesn't open you can lodge a complaint. Have a good flight and don't bother me. (*The* REPORTER *and the* PHOTOGRAPHER *lurch backwards in their seats as the plane takes off.*)

PHOTOGRAPHER: Okay, man. When the pilot dives, you push a button on the left side of your helmet.

REPORTER: What does that do?

PHOTOGRAPHER: Try it, man. You see the nozzle there? Pure oxygen! (*He takes a hit. The* REPORTER *follows suit.*) You dive. The jungle gets closer and closer like it's flying up to slam you. You can see the tree that's going to hit you, then the leaves on the tree, then the veins on the leaves—and then the pilot pulls out and he starts to climb. The sky comes crushing down on you, your eyes go black, it's like you're being crushed by darkness. Then you level off and everything goes back to normal. Then you dive again. It's outa sight.

REPORTER: Can you see the victims on the ground?

PHOTOGRAPHER: Man, you can see their *faces!* You can see the little lights coming out of the end of their machine guns. Bullets flying up at just below the speed of sound, you screaming straight down toward 'em. Hit one and you cashed your checks!

REPORTER: One bullet couldn't bring a plane down.

PHOTOGRAPHER: Man, at that speed a stiff stream of piss could bring a plane down. Hey! We're diving!

REPORTER: Wait! I haven't got my background done! What's the pilot's home town? I don't even know what the pilot's home town is!

PHOTOGRAPHER: Wooo!

REPORTER: Stop the plane! I have to do an interview!

PHOTOGRAPHER: I thought you quit.

REPORTER: I did, but—(*The plane pitches sharply as it steepens its dive.*) Oh-h-h—

PHOTOGRAPHER: Fifty meters in two seconds! Woo! This guy is good!

REPORTER: My stomach just went out with the exhaust fumes.

PHOTOGRAPHER: See that little man? Guerrilla. Look, he's waiting. Now he's lifting up his rifle.

REPORTER: Pull out!

PHOTOGRAPHER: The pilot let the bombs go. See? They're traveling down right next to us.

REPORTER: Those?

PHOTOGRAPHER: Uh-huh.

REPORTER: Those are bombs?

PHOTOGRAPHER: Yep.

REPORTER: If they slipped a half a foot they'd blow us up. They're getting closer!

PHOTOGRAPHER: Little man down there is firing!

REPORTER: (*To the bomb outside his window.*) Down there! Get him! We're your friends!

PHOTOGRAPHER: Yah! Little fucker hit the pilot! Good shot! Woo! (*He starts snapping pictures.*)

REPORTER: We're going to crash!

PHOTOGRAPHER: You bet your ass! We're going down!

REPORTER: Bail out!

PHOTOGRAPHER: You go. I'm staying. You don't think I'm gonna miss this!

REPORTER: Miss what?

PHOTOGRAPHER: When's the last time you saw shots of a plane crash taken *from the plane?*

REPORTER: I'm going! (*He "bails out."*)

PHOTOGRAPHER: Great shot of your ass, Jim! Wooo!
(*He whoops and snaps pictures as the scream of the descent increases. The stage goes black as the crash is heard —a colossal explosion. House lights up for:*)

Slide: INTERMISSION

# ACT TWO

## Slide: VILLAGE

(*Tape: the voice of the* EVENT *renders the Ambonese national anthem, which is jerry-built and grandiose. As the lights come up, an* AMBONESE PSYCHOLOGICAL WARFARE OFFICER *is taking his place in front of a group of unseen villagers. He carries a small table arrayed with assorted apparatus for the demonstration he is about to perform. A small cassette player on the table is the source of the anthem.*)

*The* REPORTER *is seated on the ground between us and the* OFFICER, *slightly off to one side. He is dressed like a villager, in black-pyjama pants, a conical hat, and sandals. By his feet is a small bundle. He is sitting on his haunches Asian-style, quite relaxed and placid, waiting for the* OFFICER *to start. The* OFFICER *clicks off the cassette.*)

OFFICER: Citizens of So Bin Village, you have done a hard day's work. The Government wishes to submit to you a presentation. (*He arranges his apparatus, which includes a bowl of rice, a basin, chopsticks, a towel, and a quart jug of thick, fetid, poisonous-looking green liquid. While he is thus employed, the* REPORTER *turns to the audience.*)

REPORTER: I drifted in my parachute what seemed like miles and miles and I landed over there. I love this village. I've been here— I don't know how long. I think this is my third week. If I had to write a dateline, I'd be out of luck. I don't, though.

OFFICER: (*Holding up the jug of green gunk.*) This is defoliant. Our friends the Americans use it to improve the jungle so our enemy cannot use it for a hiding place. The enemy has told you that this harmless liquid poisons you and makes your babies come out of your stomachs with no arms and legs. This is not so. You will see for yourself when I have poured some defoliant in this bowl. (*He does. Then "acting" stiffly.*) My but it was hot today. My face is very dirty. I have need to wash my hands and face. (*He does so, dipping and turning his hands in the green liquid, then splashing it on his face. He looks as happy as the people in TV soap commercials.*) Ah! That is refreshing! (*He wipes himself dry.*)

REPORTER: (*To the audience.*) A company of Government soldiers has been using this village as an outpost. They were here when I arrived. Today at dusk some transport choppers will be coming in to pick them up. I mean to pick *us* up. I'll catch a lift to the airbase, then a plane home. Home *America*. (*Bemusedly.*) I don't know why I said that. Home where else?

OFFICER: Mm, my hard day's work has given me an appetite. I think that I will eat some rice. No fish sauce? Very well then, I will pour on some of this. (*He pours defoliant over the bowl of rice and eats it with the chopsticks.*)

REPORTER: (*To the audience, referring to his squatting posture.*) The villagers all sit this way. I started it because my wound reopened when I hit the ground. But after you get used to it, it's really very comfortable.

OFFICER: (*Wiping his mouth.*) My! That was good! But

now my hearty meal has made me very thirsty. Ah! (*He "discovers" the defoliant again and drinks the rest of it, straight from the jug; sets the empty on the table with a bang.*) The guerrillas are liars. The Government speaks the truth. Goodbye. (*He clicks the anthem back on and, to its accompaniment, walks off with his gear.*)

REPORTER: It's very peaceful in this village. I've picked up bits and snatches of the language and I'm learning how to harvest rice. I spent the morning threshing. When you get the rhythm you can thresh all day. You slap the stalks against a board. The grains go sliding down and drop into a basket. That's all. Slap, slap, slap, slap . . . Nothing to write about there. No hook. No angle. Slap, slap, slap . . . (*A GOVERNMENT SOLDIER comes on. He is tying the legs of a chicken with a cord that hangs from his belt.*) There goes the last of the soldiers. I should go with him. Before I do, I want to show you what I've learned. (*To the SOLDIER.*) Tay dap moung. (*Translating for the audience.*) That means, "Stop please." (*To the SOLDIER, in a complimentary tone and with a gesture toward the chicken.*) Kin wau ran faun to bak im brong. (*The SOLDIER stares at him in complete incomprehension. To the audience.*) I understand the language better than I speak it. (*To the SOLDIER again, more slowly.*) Kin wau ran faun to bak im brong.

SOLDIER: *Fop nah in gao breet? Rew ksawn ep lam?*

REPORTER: (*To the SOLDIER, waving away his own words.*) Manh. (*To the audience.*) The trouble is that Ambonese has all these tones. You say the right sounds but the wrong tones and you've got a different meaning. Apparently I told him that his nose was like a bite of tree farm.

SOLDIER: (*Challengingly.*) Op feo ting ko bi dang?

REPORTER: Why? Because I *want* to speak your language.

I want to *duc fi rop* what you are saying and to *fan bo doung* to you.

SOLDIER: *Ken hip yan geh wim parn ti brong, ip yuh rat.*

REPORTER: (*To the audience.*) He says his chicken speaks his language better, and it's dead. That's an Ambonese joke.

SOLDIER: (*Indicating the* REPORTER's *clothes.*) *Fawn tip si bah?*

REPORTER: Am I a villager? Yes. Sure. Why not? *Meo.* I'm a villager. I'm happy here.

SOLDIER: *Prig paw yan tsi mah strak.*

REPORTER: You're not protecting me. I landed in a village you were occupying. *Nik kwan tap.* I wish you hadn't been here.

SOLDIER: *Wep ksi—*

REPORTER: (*Cutting him off.*) I'm not afraid of the guerrillas. *Manh kip.*

SOLDIER: *Manh kip?*

REPORTER: *Manh.* I'm not their enemy. In fact, I'd like to meet them. If you think I'm scared, you go ahead without me.

SOLDIER: *Sep?*

REPORTER: You go and catch your helicopter. I'm not leaving yet. *Ping dop.*

SOLDIER: *Ping dop?*

REPORTER: There'll be more troops through here. I can get a ride out any time. America won't disappear. *Ping dop.* Go catch your helicopter. (*The* SOLDIER *shrugs and starts out.*) Goodbye.

SOLDIER: (*Turns*). *Dik ram vi clao brong.*

REPORTER: (*Translating for himself.*) "Now you'll enjoy your chicken." Good.

SOLDIER: *Wep ksi ren—*

REPORTER: Yes, the guerrillas—?

SOLDIER: *—vi clao—*

REPORTER: "—will enjoy—"

SOLDIER: (*Points emphatically at the* REPORTER.)*—seng.* (*He goes off.*)

REPORTER: (*To the audience.*) There'll be troops coming back to the village. I won't be here long. And the guerrillas—well, all right, if I surprise them, then it's dangerous. I won't though. Probably they almost know already that I've stayed behind. They'll know before they come. And so I'll have a chance to talk to them. They'll see I'm not their enemy. (*He looks up at the sky.*) It's getting dark now. (*He crosses to his bundle and unwraps it.*) I've been sleeping over here. Sometimes it's rained, and then I've made a lean-to with my parachute. Tonight it looks like I can use it for a pillow. (*He "fluffs up" his parachute—which is mottled shades of green—and stretches out.*) I love the sky at night here. It's not a pretty sky, but it's alive. You can see the storms far off in all directions. The clouds are grey, and when the sheet lightning flashes behind them they look like flaps of dead skin, twitching. I know that that sounds ugly, but it's beautiful. (*A* GUERRILLA *comes in silently behind him.*) The guerrillas can pretend they're animals. They talk to each other in the dark that way. They also can pretend they're trees and bushes, rocks and branches, vines. Sometimes they pretend they're nothing at all. That's when you know they're near. The world is never quite that still. You don't have to tell me. This time I know he's there. (*Carefully but decisively, the* REPORTER *stands up and turns to face the* GUERRILLA. *Blackout. Tape: jungle*

*sounds—strange clicking, dripping, hissing of snakes, ani-*
*mal cries, etc.)*

## Slide: SELF-CRITICISM

(*A small, bare hut. The* REPORTER *is sleeping on the floor.*
*His head is covered by a black hood and his hands are*
*tied behind his back. A* GUERRILLA INFORMATION OFFICER
*comes in carrying a bowl of rice.*)

GUERRILLA: Stand up, please.

REPORTER: (*Coming awake.*) What?

GUERRILLA: Please stand up.

REPORTER: It's hard with hands behind the back.

GUERRILLA: I will untie them.

REPORTER: That's all right. I'll make it. (*With some clum-*
*siness, he gets to his feet.*) There I am.

GUERRILLA: I offered to untie your hands.

REPORTER: I'd just as soon you didn't. When you know
that you can trust me, then untie my hands. I'd let you
take the hood off.

GUERRILLA: (*Takes the hood off.*) Tell me why you think
that we should trust you.

REPORTER: I'm no threat to you. I've never done you any
harm.

GUERRILLA: No harm?

REPORTER: I guess I've wasted your munitions. Part of one
of your grenades wound up imbedded in my derriere—my
backside.

GUERRILLA: I speak French as well as English. You forget
—the French were here before you.

REPORTER: Yes.

GUERRILLA: You told us that you came here as a newsman.

REPORTER: Right.

GUERRILLA: You worked within the system of our enemies and subject to their interests.

REPORTER: Partly subject.

GUERRILLA: Yet you say that you have never done us any harm.

REPORTER: All I found out as a reporter was I'd never find out anything.

GUERRILLA: Do we pardon an enemy sniper if his marksmanship is poor?

REPORTER: Yes, if he's quit the army.

GUERRILLA: Ah, yes. You are not a newsman now.

REPORTER: That's right.

GUERRILLA: What are you?

REPORTER: What am I? (*The* GUERRILLA *is silent.*) I'm what you see.

GUERRILLA: What do you do?

REPORTER: I live.

GUERRILLA: You live?

REPORTER: That's all.

GUERRILLA: You live in Am-bo Land.

REPORTER: I'm here right now.

GUERRILLA: Why?

REPORTER: Why? You've got me prisoner.

GUERRILLA: If you were not a prisoner, you would not be here?

REPORTER: No.

GUERRILLA: Where would you be?

REPORTER: By this time, I'd be back in East Dubuque.

GUERRILLA: You were not leaving when we captured you.

REPORTER: I was, though. I was leaving soon.

GUERRILLA: Soon?

REPORTER: Yes.

GUERRILLA: When?

REPORTER: I don't know exactly. Sometime.

GUERRILLA: Sometime.

REPORTER: Yes.

GUERRILLA: You have no right to be here even for a minute. Not to draw one breath.

REPORTER: You have no right to tell me that. I'm here. It's where I am.

GUERRILLA: We are a spectacle to you. A land in turmoil.

REPORTER: I don't have to lie to you. Yes, that attracts me.

GUERRILLA: Yes. You love to see us kill each other.

REPORTER: No. I don't.

GUERRILLA: You said you didn't have to lie.

REPORTER: I'm not. It does—excite me that the stakes are life and death here. It makes everything—intense.

GUERRILLA: The stakes cannot be life and death unless some people die.

REPORTER: That's true. But I don't make them die. They're dying anyway.

GUERRILLA: You just watch.

REPORTER: That's right.

GUERRILLA: Your standpoint is aesthetic.

REPORTER: Yes, all right, yes.

GUERRILLA: You enjoy our situation here.

REPORTER: I'm filled with pain by things I see.

GUERRILLA: And yet you stay.

REPORTER: I'm here.

GUERRILLA: You are addicted.

REPORTER: Say I am, then! I'm addicted! Yes! I've said it! I'm addicted!

GUERRILLA: Your position in my country is morbid and decadent. It is corrupt, reactionary, and bourgeois. You have no right to live here.

REPORTER: This is where I live. You can't pass judgment.

GUERRILLA: I have not passed judgment. You are useless here. A man must give something in return for the food he eats and the living space he occupies. This is not a moral obligation but a practical necessity in a society where no one is to be exploited.

REPORTER: Am-bo Land isn't such a society, is it?

GUERRILLA: Not yet.

REPORTER: Well, I'm here right now. If you don't like that then I guess you'll have to kill me.

GUERRILLA: We would kill you as we pick the insects from the skin of a valuable animal.

REPORTER: Go ahead, then. If you're going to kill me, kill me.

GUERRILLA: We are not going to kill you.

REPORTER: Why not?

GUERRILLA: For a reason.

REPORTER: What's the reason?

GUERRILLA: We have told the leadership of TransPan-Global Wire Service when and where to leave one hundred thousand dollars for your ransom.

REPORTER: Ransom? TransPanGlobal?

GUERRILLA: Yes.

REPORTER: But that's no good. I told you, I don't work there anymore.

GUERRILLA: Your former employers have not made the separation public. We have made our offer public. You will not be abandoned in the public view. It would not be good business.

REPORTER: (*Truly frightened for the first time in the scene.*) Wait. You have to think this out. A hundred thousand dollars is too much. It's much too much. You might get ten.

GUERRILLA: We have demanded one hundred.

REPORTER: They won't pay that. Take ten thousand. That's a lot to you.

GUERRILLA: It is. But we have made our offer.

REPORTER: Change it. You're just throwing away money. Tell them ten. They'll never pay a hundred thousand.

GUERRILLA: We never change a bargaining position we have once set down. This is worth much more than ten thousand dollars or a hundred thousand dollars.

REPORTER: Please—

GUERRILLA: Sit down.

REPORTER: (*Obeys; then, quietly.*) Please don't kill me.

GUERRILLA: Do not beg your life from me. The circumstances grant your life. Your employers will pay. You will live.

REPORTER: You sound so sure.

GUERRILLA: If we were not sure we would not waste this food on you. (*He pushes the bowl of rice towards the* REPORTER.)

REPORTER: How soon will I know?

GUERRILLA: Soon. Ten days.

REPORTER: That's not soon.

GUERRILLA: This war has lasted all my life. Ten days is soon. (*Untying the* REPORTER's *hands.*) You will be fed on what our soldiers eat. You will think that we are starving you, but these are the rations on which we march toward our inevitable victory. Eat your rice. In three minutes I will tie you again. (*He goes out. The* REPORTER *eats as best he can. Blackout. Slides: the face of the* EVENT, *each frame now showing two of his features, in somewhat finer half-tone.*)

## Slide: RESCUE

(*Lights up on* MR. KINGSLEY, *seated at his desk. He is talking on the telephone.*)

KINGSLEY: Sure they're going to bring him here, but hell, Dave, you don't really want to talk to him. Why put a crimp in your imagination? Make sure you don't contradict our bulletins. Beyond that, go to town. The sky's the limit. (*The* REPORTER *appears at the door.*) Dave, I've got to sign off. Get to work on this right now, check? I'll be firing some more ideas your way as they occur to me. Over and out. (*The* REPORTER *wanders into the office. He looks blown out. He is still in his villager clothes.*) So here you are. How far they bring you?

REPORTER: Three guerrillas brought me to the border of the City. Then they gambled with some sticks. One brought me here. He's gone.

KINGSLEY: You look all shot to shit. Sit down.

REPORTER: (*Unthinkingly sits down on his haunches; then continues.*) He had the longest knife I ever saw. Strapped here, across his back. It would have gone right through me. He took off his thongs and hid them in the underbrush and put on shoes. We started through the streets. He wasn't used to shoes. They came untied. He didn't know how to tie them. So he stood still and I tied them for him. All the time he had this knife. The longest knife I ever saw. (*Pause.*) I'd have gone back out with him if he'd have let me.

KINGSLEY: How you fixed for cash?

REPORTER: I have some. (*He takes some rumpled, pale bills of different colors out of his shirt.*) Here.

KINGSLEY: I wasn't asking you to give it to me.

REPORTER: I owe it to you.

KINGSLEY: No you don't.

REPORTER: A hundred thousand dollars.

KINGSLEY: Just forget about it.

REPORTER: Am I supposed to work for you now? I can probably do some kind of work. I can't report the news.

KINGSLEY: We're square. We'll get our value for the hundred grand. You're a four-part feature. Maybe six if we can stretch it. We might try some kind of angle with a

girl guerrilla. That's a thought. (*He picks up the phone.*)
Get me Dave Feltzer again. (*To the* REPORTER.) No, all
we ask of you is don't give information to the rival press.
We want a clean exclusive. We'll be signing your name to
the story, by the way. Don't be surprised.

REPORTER: Why should I be surprised?

KINGSLEY: Well, when you read it.

REPORTER: I won't read it.

KINGSLEY: Okay. Want to catch the movie if you can.
We're trying to interest Redford. (*Into the phone.*) Yeah,
hold on, Dave. (*To the* REPORTER.) I think that's all then.

REPORTER: That's all? (*Pause.* KINGSLEY *just sits with the
phone in his hand.*) Okay. Goodbye, Bob. (*He turns and
leaves.*)

KINGSLEY: (*Into the phone.*) Yeah Dave. Got a little
brainstorm for the sequence in the punji pit. He's down
there, right, he's got this bamboo sticking through his
feet, and he looks up and sees an AK-47 clutched in little
tapered fingers and the fingernails are painted red . . .
(*Blackout. Tape: tinny Asian-Western rock-and-roll as in
Act I, Scene 4 [Strip]; this time a ballad—say, "Ruby
Tuesday.*")*

## Slide: PROPOSAL

(*Lights up on* LI's *room at the Coral Bar. A bed, a door-
way made of hanging beads, a screen.* LI *is behind the
screen, dressing. The* REPORTER *is lying on the bed. They
have just had sex. The* REPORTER *lies quietly a while before he speaks.*)

REPORTER: Li?

* See special note on copyright page.

LI: Yes?

REPORTER: It's good here. It's so good with you.

LI: (*Professionally.*) It's good with you too.

REPORTER: When I look in your eyes, your eyes look back. I love that. That's so important to me.

LI: I love that too.

REPORTER: I love to be with you.

LI: I love to be with you too.

REPORTER: Do you love me, Li? You don't, I know.

LI: I love you. Love you best of all my men.

REPORTER: Do you know what? When I come here I pretend we short-time just because we both just want to. I pretend you wouldn't take my money only Mai Wah makes you take it.

LI: Mai Wah makes me or I no take money.

REPORTER: Would you short-time me for love?

LI: Yes.

REPORTER: Are you sure you would?

LI: Yes.

REPORTER: Are you absolutely sure?

LI: Yes.

REPORTER: Li, I don't have any money.

LI: (*Emerging from behind the screen.*) What you say?

REPORTER: I'm broke. No money.

LI: No. You joke with Li.

REPORTER: I had to see you and I didn't want to spoil it by telling you till after.

LI: I have to pay myself now. Mai Wah writes it down, who comes here, how much time. Now you no pay I have to pay myself.

REPORTER: I didn't know that.

LI: Now you know.

REPORTER: I paid a lot of times, Li. Maybe it's fair that you pay once.

LI: Get out of here.

REPORTER: Li—

LI: Next time I see money first, like you G.I. I thought you nice. You trick me. You get out of here.

REPORTER: Li, marry me.

LI: What you say?

REPORTER: I say I want us to get married.

LI: Now you really joke. You bad man.

REPORTER: I'm not joking, Li. I mean it.

LI: Yes? You marry me?

REPORTER: That's right.

LI: You take me to America?

REPORTER: America? No.

LI: Marry me, not take me to America? You leave me here?

REPORTER: I stay with you, Li. I'm not going to America.

LI: You lie. Sometime you go.

REPORTER: I'm never going to go. I'm going to stay here.

LI: No. America is good. Here no good. You marry me and take me to America.

REPORTER: If I wanted to go to America, I wouldn't want to marry you.

LI: Li just good enough for Am-bo Land. You have round-eye wife, go back to her. I know.

REPORTER: You're wrong, Li. I am never going back.

LI: You say then why you want to marry me.

REPORTER: You make me feel at home here and this country *is* my home. I want to sleep with you, wake up with you. I want to look at you and see you looking back.

LI: Where you live now?

REPORTER: Well, really nowhere just this minute. See, I haven't got a job right now—

LI: You go now.

REPORTER: Wait, Li—

LI: You come back, you show me money first. You owe me for three short-times because you stay so long.

REPORTER: Li, listen—

LI: No. You go away. Not be here when I come back. (*She goes out through the beaded curtain. Blackout. Tape: a distant foghorn.*)


## Slide: WORK

(*Dim lights up on the* REPORTER. *It is dusk. He is waiting for someone.* OFFICER X *appears. He wears a stateside class-A army overcoat with the bronze oak leaves of a major on the lapels.*)

REPORTER: Officer X? Then you *are* an officer. I didn't know if that might be a code name.

X: What's with the gook suit?

REPORTER: It's just my clothes.

x: They've gotta go. Hawaiian shirts and shiny Harlem slacks is best for couriers. You have to blend in. Give me the card that Kingsley gave you. (*The* REPORTER *hands him the red-white-and-blue card from Act I, Scene 6* [*Imprintment*].) You know the number?

REPORTER: No.

x: (*Hands back the card.*) Learn it. (*The* REPORTER *starts to put the card back in his pocket.*) Learn it now. (*The* REPORTER *reads the card, trying to memorize the number. The effort of concentration is hard for him.* OFFICER X *takes the card back.*) What's the number?

REPORTER: (*With difficulty.*) 7 . . . 38 . . . 472 . . . 4.

x: Again.

REPORTER: 738 . . . 47 . . . 24.

x: (*Pockets the card.*) Remember it. Don't write it down. Here. (*He hands the* REPORTER *a packet wrapped in paper, tied with string.*)

REPORTER: What is it?

x: Don't ask what, ask where.

REPORTER: Where?

x: Lin Cho District. Tan Hoi Street. Number 72.

REPORTER: Number 72 Tan Hoi Street.

x: Better put it under your shirt. But get an overcoat with inside pockets.

REPORTER: (*Hiding the package as directed.*) I can speak some Ambonese.

x: When we need that, we have interpreters. Be back here with the money in two hours. (*The* REPORTER *starts out.*) Hold on. Do you have a weapon?

REPORTER: —Yes.

X: Let's see it. (*The* REPORTER *doesn't move.* X *takes out a handgun.*) Here.

REPORTER: That's okay.

X: You'll pay me back in trade. Here, take it.

REPORTER: I don't need it.

X: Hell you don't.

REPORTER: I don't.

X: You've got to have it.

REPORTER: I don't want it.

X: I'll just ask you one more time. You gonna take the pistol? (*The* REPORTER *looks at it but doesn't answer.*) Give me back the package.

REPORTER: I can get it where it's going.

X: Give it.

REPORTER: Number 72 Tan Hoi—

X: Nobody carries goods for me unless they're able to protect them.

REPORTER: I'll protect them.

X: If you won't use the gun, don't think I won't. (*He points the pistol at the* REPORTER. *The* REPORTER *gives him the packet.*)

REPORTER: I can speak some Ambonese.

X: You told me. What's my number?

REPORTER: 7 . . . 7 . . . 38 . . . 738 . . . (*His face goes blank.*)

X: Good. Don't remember it again. (*He leaves the way he came. Blackout. Tape: babies crying.*)

Slide: ORPHANAGE

(*The crying of the babies continues into the scene.
Lights come up on an* Ambonese Nun *tending children
who are imagined to be in a long row of cribs between
her and the audience. The* Reporter *comes in left.*)

REPORTER: Excuse me, Sister.

NUN: Yes?

REPORTER: The Mother Superior told me to come up here.

NUN: Yes?

REPORTER: I'm going to adopt a child.

NUN: (*Scanning his garments; gently.*) Adopt a child?

REPORTER: Yes.

NUN: Have you been interviewed?

REPORTER: Not yet. I have to get a bit more settled first.
But the Mother Superior said I could come upstairs and if
I chose a child she would keep it for me.

NUN: Ah. How old a child would you want?

REPORTER: He should probably not be very young. And
tough. He should be tough. I don't have lots of money.

NUN: You said "he."

REPORTER: A girl would be all right. A girl would be nice.

NUN: It must be a girl. The Government has a law that
only girls may be adopted. The boys are wards of the
State. When they are older, they will go into the army.

REPORTER: Well, a girl is fine.

NUN: (*Starting down the line with him, moving left.*)
This girl is healthy.

REPORTER: Hello. You're very pretty. You have cheek-bones like a grownup, like your mommy must have had. Look. If I pull back my skin as tight as I can, I still don't have skin as tight as you. (*He pulls his skin back toward his temples. One effect is that this gives him slanted eyes.*) Why won't you look at me?

NUN: She is looking at you.

REPORTER: She doesn't trust me. (*To the child.*) I won't hurt you. I just want to have a child of your country. Will you be my child? (*To the* NUN.) She doesn't like me. Do you see that child down the line there? (*Pointing right.*) That one's looking at me. Let's go talk to that child.

NUN: That section is boys. This way. (*She leads him to the next crib to the left.*)

REPORTER: She's asleep but, look, her little fists are clenched. She wouldn't like me. I don't want to wake her up.

NUN: Here is another.

REPORTER: (*To the third child.*) Do you like me? I'll take care of you. I understand that you need food, and I'll try and be a friend to you. (*To the* NUN.) She doesn't even hear my voice.

NUN: Here.

REPORTER: These aren't children! These are ancient people, shrunken down! Look at their eyes! They've looked at everything! They'll never look at me!

NUN: You're upsetting the children.

REPORTER: (*Pointing toward the boys' section.*) That child sees me. He's been looking at me since I came in the room. I want that child.

NUN: I've told you that you cannot have a boy—. Wait. Which child?

REPORTER: The one who's standing up and looking at me.

NUN: The child in green?

REPORTER: Yes.

NUN: You can have the child in green. The Government will not object to that. The boy is blind.

REPORTER: Blind?

NUN: Yes.

REPORTER: He isn't blind. He's looking at me.

NUN: He can't see you.

REPORTER: Yes he can.

NUN: He can't.

REPORTER: That child's the only one who sees me. How can he be blind?

NUN: He can't see.

REPORTER: He's looking at me! Can't you see? He's looking at me!

NUN: You'd better go now. Come back when you have made an application and have been approved. The boy will be here.

REPORTER: He's blind.

NUN: Yes.

REPORTER: I'm going to go now. (*He doesn't move.*)

NUN: Yes, please go now.

REPORTER: He's blind. (*He starts out the way he came.*)

NUN: God be with you. (*Blackout.*)

Slide: HOME

(*A street in the City. It is dead of night. The* REPORTER *is walking along the street. He is nearly stumbling from exhaustion. When the lights come up, it is as if—from the* REPORTER'S *point of view—they came up on the audience. He looks at the audience quizzically.*)

REPORTER: Hello. You look familiar. I believe I used to talk to you. Are you my readers? I'm doing very well. Last night I found a refrigerator carton that would shelter a whole family with their pigs and chickens. Next to it a trash pile I can live off for a week. If I can find my way back. I kind of get lost on these streets sometimes. (*Pause.*) Sometimes I can stand like this and drift in all directions through the City, soaking up the sounds . . . (*Sitting down on the pavement.*) There's a firefight out there beyond the border of the City. Tracers from a helicopter gunship, see, they're streaming down like water from a hose. Green tracers coming up to meet them now, they climb up towards the ship and then they drop and their green fire goes out. They fall and hit some tree somewhere. The lumber industry is almost dead in Am-bo Land. A fact I read. The trees are all so full of metal that the lumber mills just break their sawblades. (*The lights take on bodiless whiteness.*) Magnesium flares. They're floating down on little parachutes. I floated down like that once. Everything is turning silver and the shadows are growing and growing. The street looks like the surface of the moon. And listen. (*The* EVENT'S *voice, on tape, has come softly on: elusive Asian music from the opening titles of the play. The* REPORTER *shuts his eyes. As the sounds continue, he falls into a position almost too awkward to be sleep; a position that suggests a drunken stupor or a state of shock. The* EVENT *makes more sounds, blending them together almost soothingly: a helicopter passing overhead; distant mortar and automatic weapons fire; more Asian music, very lulling. From far along the street is heard the creaking sound of dolly wheels. The* Photographer *comes on, now legless, propelling himself on a platform.*)

Photographer: Hey, is that a body, man? God damn, a Yankee dressed up like a gook. Yeah, that's a picture. Hold it. Smile, Charlie. (*He takes a flash photo. Simultaneously with the flash, the stage goes black and the picture appears on the screen. It is the head and shoulders of a body in the same position as the* Reporter's, *and dressed identically. The face is that of the* Event. *The picture holds for several seconds, then clicks off.*)

Slide: HOW I GOT THAT STORY

END